Smuggling Elephants
through
Airport Security

Smuggling Elephants through Airport Security

POEMS BY **BRAD JOHNSON**

WHEELBARROW BOOKS ▪ *East Lansing*

∞ The paper used in this publication meets the minimum requirements of ANSI/NISO z39.48-1992 (R 1997) (Permanence of Paper).

Wheelbarrow Books
Michigan State University Press
East Lansing, Michigan 48823-5245

Printed and bound in the United States of America.

29 28 27 26 25 24 23 22 21 20   1 2 3 4 5 6 7 8 9 10

Library of Congress Control Number: 2019905123
ISBN 978-1-61186-353-6 (paper)
ISBN 978-1-60917-627-3 (PDF)
ISBN 978-1-62895-389-3 (ePub)
ISBN 978-1-62896-390-8 (Kindle)

Book design by Charlie Sharp, Sharp Des!gns, East Lansing, MI
Cover design by Erin Kirk New
Cover art by Taylor Meers Jacobs

green press INITIATIVE Michigan State University Press is a member of the Green Press Initiative and is committed to developing and encouraging ecologically responsible publishing practices. For more information about the Green Press Initiative and the use of recycled paper in book publishing, please visit *www.greenpressinitiative.org.*

Visit Michigan State University Press at *www.msupress.org*

With the publication of Brad Johnson's *Smuggling Elephants through Airport Security,* the Residential College in the Arts and Humanities (RCAH) Center for Poetry at Michigan State University offers its fifth book in our Wheelbarrow Books Poetry Series. Clearly, we pay homage to William Carlos Williams and his iconic poem, "The Red Wheelbarrow." Readers will remember the poem begins with, "so much depends upon . . ." that red wheelbarrow. As spring tries to remember how to make its way back to Michigan, I am thinking of the wonderful way poetry brings together the overlap of our emotional seasons.

There is snow on the ground here, and it's 12 degrees. But it's also March, the month that brings us the spring equinox. *Smuggling Elephants through Airport Security* (how could you not take a book from the shelf with that title?) juxtaposes the dreaded trek through TSA officials with the marvelously whimsical idea of getting by those lobby cops with Jumbo or Horton. Poets delight us with new images, new ways of thinking and being in the world. They move us from the mundane to the mysterious, the improbable to the possible.

We are at a critical time in the history of our country, and the world, where we need to stand up for the sanctity of the word. We need to understand how language both warps truth and how it defends truth, how poetry utters truths that political speeches and rhetorical flourishes cannot, how poetry evokes in us that which is most human, most universal, and most personal. It gives us Billy Collins' bread and knife, Robert Hayden's winter Sundays, Elizabeth Bishop's waiting room, Margaret Atwood's variations on the word *sleep.* At the end of her poem, "Summer Day," the late Mary Oliver asks us to think about the question which we all, regardless of race, religion, ethnicity, gender, economic situation or geographical location, ask in the darkness of the night and in moments of bewilderment or despair: ". . . what is it you plan to do with your one wild and precious life?" Poetry helps us answer that question by providing a retreat, a place of stillness and contemplation, a place of safety and inspiration. It allows for the smuggling of elephants.

As our number of Wheelbarrow Books increases, we hope that our audience increases also. Help us spread the word. In the beginning was the word, and the word became the poem. So much depends upon the collaboration of reader, writer, and poem, the intimate ways we come to know one another. So much depends upon this relationship.

—ANITA SKEEN, *Wheelbarrow Books Series Editor*

Brad Johnson's *Smuggling Elephants through Airport Security* is a kaleidoscopic tour of the American moment, as conducted by a poet unafraid of the vertiginous highs and lows of a culture that sends into collision its smart cars, hurricanes, emojis, pop heroes, meth houses, TV pundits, rock stars and refugees. This moment, he writes, is the *rising tropical storm surge of American's second antebellum*. One reads these voicings of our collective bewilderment with a frisson of recognition: the present has never seemed more unpredictable and portentous, the future more uncertain. Johnson writes playfully and poignantly about his children, who make cameo appearances schooling their teacher about evolution; his daughter *mutes alarm clocks just by pointing at them*. His surrealism resides in the blur of absurdities with deeply political ramifications. The secret to the title is revealed by an incident in an airport having to do with a belt buckle shaped like a revolver, and its genius is its argument regarding the thingness of things. The tutelary spirit of this work could easily have been John Ashbery. I have not encountered many poets as brave as Johnson, as willing to go anywhere and see what happens, all the while imagining that even here, even now, it is possible to find one's way.

—CAROLYN FORCHÉ

Contents

Smuggling Elephants through Airport Security

Sunset

When Bill O'Reilly tells Dennis Miller about his visit
to Gitmo, he recounts how there was an arrow pointing
towards Mecca, the direction which they should pray,
drawn on the walls of the Muslim prisoners' cells
but the American guards erased the arrows and redrew
them pointing towards Las Vegas. O'Reilly thought
this was cool. Vito turns to me and says he thought
it was cool when atheists transformed the greeting
Merry Christmas to *Happy Holidays* and O'Reilly's head
exploded. Vito lives a block from where Axl Rose shot
heroin back in the eighties but we still drive to Sunset
to park near where The Doors dragged Jim Morrison
into Whiskey A Go Go wearing only cowboy boots
and underpants. In Morrison's last photographs, five years
later, he's dressed in pink collared shirt with blue sweater tied
around his neck like he's waiting for his doubles partner
outside some private Connecticut tennis club. Across
from Whiskey A Go Go there's a Subway now. Vito shows
me where the hookers used to bend into unrolled
windows of slowed sedans. Maybe the west isn't the west
anymore. Maybe it moved north to Seattle in the nineties
with Pearl Jam, Mudhoney and Sleater-Kinney, only to scatter
to Nashville, Omaha and Brooklyn like shotgun spray
after Cobain's suicide, and never returned. Vito points
east where tourists walk on names of fallen stars. Back
at his apartment we watch a CNN report on how climate change
wobbled the Earth into a new rotation so maybe west
really isn't west and we're all north-northwest, kneeling
before chosen altars, faces burned by southerly wind.

Living by the Sword

Saif migrated from Iraq after his father was killed
in one of the bombings. When his girlfriend calls,
I listen on speakerphone and I don't know if it's her voice
or the Arabic she speaks that's beautiful so after he hangs up
I tell him I could listen to them talk all day in a language
I don't understand and Saif says he uses only a fraction
of Arabic since its so specific. *For example,* he says,
we don't say "camel." There's not one word for camel.
There's a word for "old camel" and "young camel."
A different word for "the camel on the left drinking
from the river" and "the camel on the left drinking
from the stream" and "the camel on the right drinking
from the stream" and "the pregnant camel on the right that drank
from the stream and then went to the river for more."
There's five-hundred million words in Arabic, compared
to a million in English and we only use a fraction.
Good thing there's no camels in Los Angeles, I tell him.

I want to apologize for America not being a melting pot
or a tossed salad but an eight-dollar smoothie, blended
by violence, puréed by whirling blades but Saif says
he loves it here. Everyone accepts his identity.
Before I suggest this may not be acceptance but apathy
he says it's wonderful to be able to disagree and not worry
about being beheaded by some hypocrite who knows
he'd never do anything worth being beheaded for but sizes up
everyone else's neck. *No one is aware of their own hypocrisy*
in the Middle East, he says. But Saif believes in Sharia Law,
that thieves should lose a hand as punishment, rapists
an arm and a leg, believes this serves as effective deterrence.
Americans don't get this, he says. *Jails and prisons supply*
food and showers. This is a reward. But what if you're wrong?

I ask. What if you chop off an arm and the accuser later
recants: *It was not this man. I made a mistake.*

Innocent and guilty. Innocence and guilt. These are words,
Saif says. How many words in Arabic are there for innocent?
His girlfriend calls again and I still don't know if it's her voice
or the sound of her voice through the speakerphone speaking
Arabic but I'm in love with the sound. When he hangs up,
he says, *You know my name, Saif, it translates into sword.*
I don't ask what kind. There's so many different types of swords.

Meeting Osama

My daughter introduces me to Osama
in the parking lot outside her school
during aftercare pickup. I've heard
about his parents, their immigration
from Baghdad a year ago after losing
their house during the peace after the war.
They moved into our neighborhood.
Now their son, Osama, occupies a desk
three over from my daughter in first grade.

Since he's in my daughter's class
that means he was probably born
in '07, years after his namesake brought
down the sky. But maybe Osama's
a family name for an honored child;
perhaps his grandfather, Osama, directed
military action against Iran in 1988;
or his oldest uncle, Osama, designed
the most famous of Iraq's palace porticos.

I have many German friends but never met an Adolph.

O, the burden of naming children!
O, the weight of another's name!

When my daughter calls him Osama
I flinch, even as I worry for him
and hope he has the sense to stick
to cities as he ages and not stray
into American gun country where
all Osamas will always be the same
Osama even though *that* Osama's dead.

I'm thinking this as my daughter wraps
her arm around little Osama's shoulder
and whispers in his ear, prompting
him to announce he can turn himself
invisible. Then my daughter looks
at me and laughs as we watch him close
his eyes and squeeze them into lines.

A Whole Lot of Patience and Time

After watching the politician deliver the campaign's
best speech after losing the Florida primary and dropping
from the presidential race, we argue over differences
between conservative and liberal, how perhaps republicanism
is the closest we'll ever get to democracy. He insists
essence precedes existence, that truth is a universal
not a relative construct. I believe in relativism
but do admit to innate feelings of wrong and right
whose seed I can't locate, the planter I can't identify.
I give the example of my daughter's report
on George Harrison for her music class, how the day
after I help her complete the assignment I hear
Got My Mind Set on You for the first time in more
than twenty years on satellite radio driving her to school.
How should I explain the connectedness I feel
when happenings like this occur or when the morning
following this conversation about synchronicity
and George Harrison another George Harrison song plays
on satellite radio en route to my daughter's school?
I want there to be some connection other than me
between this song and that discussion and universal truth
and my daughter and I want this connection to mean
more than only my observing it but I also want orioles,
cardinals and jays outside my daughter's school filling
the tops of the autumn oak trees with oranges, blues
and reds but when we pull up there's just a small murder
of common crows pecking through the parking lot debris.

Buddha Looking Thin

I've always found undue comfort in knowing
so I ask the woman standing in line
at the Boca Raton Marshalls wearing
yoga pants and Buddha T-shirt to which aspect
of Buddha she most relates: the wealthy,
aristocratic pre-Buddha Buddha or Buddha starving
for nirvana beneath the Bodhi tree? I ask
if she believes a T-shirt manufactured
by exploited labor violates the Eightfold Path
or if she feels Americans make choices
and once across the river on Buddha's raft leave
the raft behind, free to embrace consumerism
but she looks at me like I'm a weirdo
for commenting on a shirt she probably bought
on sale and never thought about again.
I'm not sure if that makes her more enlightened
or less and wonder if there's a scale anywhere
accurate in measuring such things.

Archaeology of Silence

Can we assume the bald man dresses
himself in a skin-colored turtleneck
to intentionally resemble a phallus
or must he announce he's studied Freud?

When she suggests I think outside the box
I respond that saying *think outside the box*
is an example of thinking inside the box.

She looks at me like I'm French Canadian,
her eyes dull as tulip bulbs that never bloomed,
and claims I resemble Connecticut:
my best quality's my proximity to New York.

Her diction's as crowded as Wal-Mart's parking lot
on Sunday but the more she talks
the less I listen, my protests pointless
as pockets in an infant's pajama pants.

It's better not to admit the thoughts
double-parked in my brain extend to:

> *There's an awful lot of wrinkles in these wrinkle free pants.*
> *It's probably the creamer but this coffee tastes like crayon.*
> *Should I tip the delivery drone and wish it a good weekend?*

We're all geniuses when we're quiet.

> *Should I join a gym to look like a guy who goes to the gym?*
> *Do I purchase fireworks from the man with three fingers on*
> *   his right hand?*
> *The miracle of miracles is people believe in miracles.*

Sometimes silence is the stone shown
but never thrown. Still, we honor the artist,
not the art; credit the rebel who hurled
the rock with heroism, never the rock itself.

Shaken, Not Stirred

Driving home my wife reminds me of what
my mother always said: don't talk about politics
or religion in polite company but how can I not?
When I ask *what's for dinner?* the response's
always singed. Vegetarian lasagna. Free-range chicken.
Kobe beef. Foie gras. Hummus. Shark steak. Venison.
Quinoa. There's even a difference between tap water
and bottled. Maybe the hosts have separate
refrigerators, one for meat, one for dairy. Maybe
the husband cooks. Maybe the wife drinks potato vodka.
Or there's bacon served. Or bacon not served.

When Jeffrey showed up late how could I not ask
what happened and when he said he walked

how could I not follow up with *why would you walk
this time of night this time of year?* though I knew
any answer he'd supply would be dogmatic or political
like he didn't own a car and his bicycle had a flat tire
or it was Shabbat or he was protesting a prisoner's release.

What answer could there possibly be, I ask my wife
as I turn off our highway exit, that wouldn't seep
into the dark corners of socially accepted conversation?
It's a beautiful night she says while placing her left hand
on mine and pushing the automatic window button
with the other. *It's a beautiful night* she repeats as wind lifts
her hair like balloons released from a net at a rally.

Ghostly Demarcations

Just because we pay to see the Pixies play
their summer concert and hear *the devil is six*
and *your mouth is everywhere* doesn't mean
the bassist playing Kim Deal's bass lines
is Kim Deal or the woman singing *Gigantic,*
mimicking *a big, big love; a big, big love*
in Kim Deal's ethereal whisper and wail is Kim Deal
because Kim Deal's kicking back in Dayton
with her twin sister and a garage full of guitars.

She's back in Dayton where America's heart
has been replaced with a lawnmower engine,
where the Wright brothers' childhood home
is housed in what is now considered flyover
country. Just because we're on the lawn
at the Pixies show listening to them perform
Debaser while Kim Deal is back in Dayton
again doesn't mean we prefer the counterfeit
to the authentic or that we can't recognize
backyard sprinklers crying when it rains.

The Factory

Rachel shows me the Brillo box snow globe
she bought from the Andy Warhol Museum
gift shop last time she was home and tells me
they had a Velvet Underground room that closed
due to little traffic and lack of interest which is why
I think Warhol left Pittsburgh for New York
in the first place, to deliver himself from that repressive
Midwestern provincialism in order to surround himself
with people who valued his vision, his replication
of American things like soup cans and Brillo boxes
and Elvis that were not soup cans, Brillo boxes or Elvis.

When President Trump tweets about being
president of Pittsburgh, not Paris, he's referring
to the Pittsburgh of the 20th century, of smoke stacks
and steel workers and coal mines where I got
mugged at 2 a.m. outside the Greyhound station
escaping Detroit for Baltimore circa 1990.
The president's not talking about governing
today's Pittsburgh with its craft beer houses,
vegetarian restaurants and dropping crime rate.

It's impossible to know which Pittsburgh
someone's referencing when they mention it
which must have been the same for Warhol's mother
who, when she read about her son in *Time* magazine
back in 1967, must have been so proud to learn
Andy was making an honest, Midwestern living
working long hours in a factory of his own creation.

Where Late the Sweet Birds Sang

Twin Buddha statues grin and grab
their fat bellies in our backyard
garden as the smell of lemons
ground in the garbage disposal
dances through the screen door
like the D. H. Lawrence of Detroit.

Every passing Ford grins
its father's smiling grill, stares
with its mother's headlight eyes
while a surprise symphony erupts
from our cocker spaniel's snore.
Motor oil stains our driveway
in the shape of a fleur-de-lis.

It's autumn already: the city
bankrupt, Tiger Stadium torn
down. Our invitations include
warnings now. Every year more
move away; fewer move in.
It's hard to tell hovels from homes
in Highland Park where grandma
lived and her doctor dad made
house calls. Soon they'll build
another casino along the river.

The neighbor's Labrador licks
water from its porch bowl
as my fingers trace along your arm
like veins of rain trailing up
a highway windshield on I-75.
Even as we touch I'm nostalgic

for your skin as if the process
of touching is the first step
in letting go. There's no deeper
than the deepest. Your goodnight
kiss is as syrupy as the raspberry
popsicle melting on the counter.

Our scars were inflicted, here,
in the kitchen and there's a lesson
in the laundry: everything bleeds.

Zen and the Art of Blowing Off Friends

We aren't climbing Everest or hiking
Calcutta or dropping out from the door
of an open plane, just off-road biking
or loitering inside the Apple store.
But when Harold joins, he always complains
about the heat or his health unravels
which happens whenever we're hit with rain.
Harold says he never needs to travel.
He'd rather stay home sipping chianti
than go out for a beer or a game. He
swears Heaven's his porch in Ypsilanti,
and if he found heaven why would he leave?
"We're all going to die," I once tried to push.
"You're right," he replied, "but there is no rush."

Jonah and the Tractor

My father says *this is not a war; this is a negotiation*
and I want to believe but we're fighting over who I was
and what I've come to be. And who returns to Ohio
after living in New York City? Besides, my bedroom's
now an office, my trophies boxed on basement shelves.
What does the future owe the past? What does America
owe the Midwest? My hopes are small as sparrows resting
on the rotting row of fence dividing our field from the line
of Amish homes blooming along the river. Jonah interrupts
my father's assault with a double knock on the aluminum
screen door. The last I saw him was years before I heard
about his tractor tipping into the drainage ditch, tumbling
down the ravine like a candy wrapper twisting in the wind.
Perched against the newly painted porch column, he claims
the violence of his amputation was almost gentle, says
his absent space of arm is now thick with presence. He talks
about teaching himself to use his hip when lifting bails
of hay; his knees to balance a steering wheel when shifting
gears; his teeth to grip a bottle opener to pop a top, making
him popular at local parties. Then he focuses on a single
weed stretching out of the potted geranium hanging
from the ceiling like it's a stranger trespassing on his farm.
He rips it to the root, tosses the clump of soil into the front
yard garden, settles back against the column and looks
at me like *I'm* the stranger crossing his property or the weed
usurping nutrients from a decorative flower and says
that sometimes, in the morning, after he pins his sleeve
near his shoulder when getting dressed he half-expects
the thing to sprout anew like an iguana tail or asparagus stalk
or something that returns but can't recall ever being gone.

How the Other Half Lives

Half the residents of Florida are fools
who spend upwards of $50,000 on shatter-proof window glass,
$20,000 on accordion shutters or invest three to five
hours slicing appendages, twisting knee and elbow joints
on ladders in high, last minute winds while installing
steel shutter panels with wing nuts. Or they pay
random dudes a thousand dollars cash to put
the shutters up and another thousand to take them down.

The other half, like reverse Cassandras, insists
the worst won't hit, refer to the storm map
as conjecture and theorize that hurricane-category wind
won't extend further than 40 miles outside
the eye and we'll be well outside the cone.

Megan's front doors burst in and the neighbor's bike flew
into the living room as though flung by a giant.
Beneath a mattress in her parents' bathtub she gripped
its swollen edges like a parachute every time the storm sucked
breath from their, now, roofless home. She considered
praying but the wind would only erase her voice.

Dumb Gary walked his wife's Bichon during the eye
thinking the storm passed. He whispered how lucky
he felt living on the west side of the street; the side
where none of the pool enclosures collapsed.
I didn't tell him we're in the eye, that the winds
will be reversing, the storm returning back for his screen
but watched, three hours later, as he lifts the arms
of the aluminum framing from his pool like masts from some half-sunk
clipper ship, the black screens soaked like torn sails.

Under a hurricane warning, 36 hours before the winds,
the shelves of liquor stores empty of tequila before Wal-Mart starts
rationing cases of water, before the gas station pumps
run dry. After the storm, half of all Floridians drink
from the punch bowl of schadenfreude as they bicycle
through their neighborhoods evaluating the damage
or lack thereof. Half of Floridians are fools
but it's impossible to tell which half until after the storm wobbles
west or speeds north toward the Carolinas.

Florida Man

I would trade the entire Rolling Stones and remaining
members of The Who if we could've kept Tom Petty
but I admit this math is weird. If we're preventing Texas
from seceding in order to keep Austin part of America
and forgiving Georgia since it's home to Athens and Atlanta
perhaps Tom Petty being born and meeting Elvis in Gainesville's
enough to redeem the entire state of Florida; a state that teases
tourists in Creole, Hebrew, Portuguese, French, Russian,
Ukrainian or some pidgin in between, and nine Spanish dialects
similar enough to be related but too idiosyncratic to make it
through dinner without fighting over which loves their mother more;
a state that presides in Everglades courtrooms, hearing arguments
made by alligators, pythons and armadillos over squatter's rights
and eminent domain; a state of turnover chains and Ponzi schemes,
hanging chads and Al Gore, the sinewy bones of mangrove fingers,
Luther Campbell and Bobby Bowden, jet skis scaring
manatees, Hemingway's six-toed cats, suburbias saturated
with the fecundity of rotting mangoes fallen from backyard trees;
a state with large shells abandoned along its chest like hats
tossed during last night's New Year's celebration, lines cracked
across their crowns by farmers to suck out the conch meat;
a state renowned for its beaches but imports its sand;
a state that's a mash-up on I-95 of *Driving Miss Daisy,*
Grand Theft Auto, Apocalypse Now; a state that repaints
retired school buses and fills them with migrant workers
to deliver, early morning, to the groves; a state whose sun purples
newsprint and plasters it across sidewalk pavements;
a state whose Florida Man won a Darwin Award after being arrested
three times, charged with public indecency and sexually assaulting
the same fold-out couch in a series of separate but strangely
singular occurrences; a state whose meth houses explode
into starless night like a 1,000 validated stereotypes

while 200 miles south dry drunks argue over lemonade,
in the last of the Tiki Hut shade, if Buddy Holly's alma mater
was your rival school might you consider switching allegiances.
One shouts to another *you can blame me for asking the question*
but not for the answer you give before nodding off, knee-deep
in the rising tropical storm surge of America's second antebellum.

They Said It Was a Weather Balloon

Eileen's daughter holds *Happy Birthday* balloons
at the bus stop when I drop off my daughter.
When I wish her happy birthday Eileen tells me
it's not her birthday. She just found the balloons
and has been carrying them with her for three days
smiling as everyone who passes wishes her happy birthday.

But as the bus pulls away she releases the string
to wave it good-bye and she cries as they lift
into the sky as the sun begins to scald the edges
of the morning clouds. *Oh no,* says Eileen.
The turtles and the manatees. When I look
to the sky I only see balloons. Not turtles. Not manatees.
Eileen sees balloons not as they are but as they'll be,
as deflating foil and latex sinking into the ocean,
suffocating the animals at home in those silent seas.

I think of how a thing is a thing but also other things,
how we try and say what we mean with language
but words are as imprecise as a drunk sniper taking
aim atop a spinning carousel and how Ezra Pound used
fifteen languages in *The Cantos* in order to employ
the correct word to perfectly express his meaning,
deciding the three rippled hieroglyph best expressed water.

As I'm walking home my wife texts me an eggplant emoji
and I can't tell if this is a sexual advance or a request
to stop at the vegan grocery. Should I respond
with a thumbs up image or a meme of frustrated Nicolas Cage?

So much depends on whether the red wheelbarrow
is just a wheelbarrow or a symbol of American industrialism.

Behind the bushes of a neighbor's house I think
I spy a giant great blue heron but it's just a stupid
black smart car parked in their driveway.

Cronus Complains of Chronic Migraines

When calluses cake my heels and palms like leavened
bread we bring my daughter home with knuckles dimpled
pink and little, loaf-like legs and she's an open window refreshing
stale basement air. My parents claim to see my wife in her.
My in-laws swear her nose is mine. Now she doesn't want
to brush her teeth. Instead, she'll insist she did so we provide
the dry toothbrush as evidence. She learns to wet the toothbrush.
Some mornings we'll discover her toothbrush still topped
with toothpaste beside the sink or find her not brushing but rubbing
toothpaste off under the faucet water with her thumb. She asks me
how to lie. I tell her she must stop smiling. It gives the truth
away. My wife and I debate having another child. The thought
of not makes us feel like murderers. When his face appears
it's inevitable. We immediately recognize him as ours. His first week
home we watch him flinch in his sleep as though he's reliving
some past life where he's hero or villain born into a home
whose humble owners suspect they should have installed
reinforced beams. My daughter says he's so cute she wants
to eat his face. We teach her to be gentle but she admits
when he turns four she plans to kick his butt. When I play
video of my infant son laughing for my infant son he reaches
for my phone in what I expect to be his first sense of self-recognition
but when he grabs the phone instead of examining the video
where his giggles turn to cackles he shoves the phone in his mouth
and chews away until drool runs down. At the beach my daughter brings
us palms full of ocean foam as my son destroys the castle we've shaped
with shovel and wet sand like some colossal berserker, stomping
the outer walls, crushing towers between his fingers. Buttresses
collapse and peasants flee the front gate as this raging titan dumps
collected shells from his plastic bucket, flooding the ramparts with debris.

Considering the Temporary at the Contemporary

As we approach the Magic Kingdom,
the Contemporary Resort appears to collapse
before us like a shoebox soaked in rain.
I tell my daughter how Disney's monorail represented
the future when I was young, how I believed
magnetic trains would be zippered
across the country's chest. She's not impressed.
Now the monorail's just another symbol
of the future become symbol of the past.

When the monorail doors automatically open
at the Contemporary, mothers push
their daughters in their puffy princess dresses aboard,
fathers angle their stroller's wheels between
our legs and I whiff my father's after shave
which reminds me of how he'd stand
in our Baltimore bathroom slapping
his reddened skin between diesel coughing fits.
He sits in front of me but I think about him then.

As the pinnacle of Cinderella's castle separates
from the cypress tops, my mother locates
Spanish moss hanging like shawls off
the cypress's bony arms and shoulders.
When I say *it's beautiful* she says *it kills the trees*
which makes me feel dumb as a dog staring
at his master's finger instead of where it's pointing.

Whispering to Captains

In line for Peter Pan's Flight at Disney World
a bunch of dudes in Deadpool T-shirts sweat
with their kids and their backpacks while tinkering
with smartphones and tablets and ignoring
the painted shields and decorative frames.

We visited Universal Studios yesterday
which had the great advantage of building
its park years after studying the flaws
in Disney's properties so we left our minivan
in the King Kong lot of a multilevel garage,
were cooled by fans installed along the sidewalks,
didn't wait in line to get photographed
with Bullwinkle or Woody Woodpecker
and now it's strange consuming Disney World
with Jewish children considering Walt's Nazi sympathies
but perhaps the lesson is it's okay to separate art
from the artist and appreciate them as different things
but Danny won't watch *Game of Thrones*
because he thinks the show betrays the books
and my brother says you can't separate
the statue from the stone from which it's carved.

The couple in line ahead of us agrees
Phish was better when Trey was shooting heroin
as Danny asks my sister if the face he sees
in an orange rind resembles Jesus or Pablo Escobar,
my son picks up a yellow Crayon wrapper he mistook
for a rolled and flattened twenty dollar bill
and my daughter whines about how unfair
my wife and I are for refusing to allow her
to have her own YouTube channel.

If all your friends are busy making
videos, we ask her, *who's left to watch them?*

Back at the hotel my son bathes
in a tub of soapy water playing
with the plastic soap wrappers, whispering
to the captains of these imaginary ships
that float in his wake before sinking.

Baltimore, in Perpetuity

It's morning and my younger brother lectures
me on the Heisenberg Principle, how
a thing is always moving, how the more
we know about where it's going the less
we know about where it is and vice versa
which makes me think of Gary Shtenyngart's claim:

To write a book set in the present
is to write about the distant past.

When I lift my nephew over
my head my brother watches me
as though he owns the store from which I'm planning
to shoplift. He remembers me stealing
twenties from our mother's wallet, wrestling
police against the line of pay phones outside
Towson Town Center, hanging
out the passenger window smashing
mailboxes with a wooden bat as Phil Alexander sped
his Honda over suburban hills of northern Maryland.

Meanwhile, my nephew laughs
and drools above me, his arms outstretched
like 737s he watches land at BWI.

Smuggling Elephants through Airport Security

Audrey and her husband pick us up
at LaGuardia and ask how our flight was.
I tell them about going through security
in Fort Lauderdale, how the belt buckle
my mom gave me for my birthday shaped
like a revolver's cylinder looked suspicious,
like a weapon, to the TSA agent and how I spent
the time it took my wife to be x-rayed
and re-shoed explaining how the buckle was meant
to look like a revolver but was not,
in fact, a gun. To illustrate my point I showed
the agent the yellow elephant my son crayoned
on green construction paper during the drive
to the airport. *Elephants*, I said, *are not allowed*
through security. Then I pointed to the picture
my son drew, insisting: *But a representation*
of a thing is not the thing. This is not an elephant.
The agent said he understood my buckle
wasn't real but warned how replicas might be
mistaken for authentic by agents at different
terminals. I tell Audrey how odd it felt
debating Plato, arguing about shadows projected
on cave walls in an American airport when
her husband in the backseat says he knows
exactly what I mean. When they last travelled
through Hartford, TSA confiscated their son's Play-Doh,
claiming it resembled explosive clay.

Robert Kraft, Owner of the New England Patriots, Accuses Vladimir Putin of StealingHis Super Bowl Ring

I've been advised not to ask for its return.
The Department of Defense discourages travel
to Russia, even Moscow, now that you support
Syria but this is not a game. As you pushed
my ring over your knuckle you laughed
and said *I could kill a man with this ring.*
Should I have taken this as confession or threat?
Then you unscrewed and pocketed it
as though it were the mobile number
of some Lithuanian hostess. Your guards corseted
themselves around you. And me, only up
to their chins. Now you're silent as an Orthodox church
after the Pussy Riot arrests. When you visited
the UN, you didn't even call. If you really thought
the ring was a gift surely you'd treat me better
than a busboy or some Bolshevik locked
away in a Siberian gulag. It's not about the money.
What's 25,000 to men like us? You were president.
Now you're czar. I've seen the photos of you, always
shirtless, on horseback, big-game hunting
with arrow quiver and compound bow, crossing
a stream with wide, bivouac smile. We've so much
in common. I'm a widower. You're divorced. We love
pretty girls dancing in bikinis, tasting
sun tan lotion in their sweat. Should I believe
the senator who claims no former KGB has soul
or my president who saw it in your eyes?
I would have introduced you to Tom and Gisele.
Now evidence of my Patriots victory is housed
in some Kremlin storage facility, forgotten
like the Cold War. I doubt you even wear it.

Northern Aggression

Like a rainbow trout caught in over-fished waters,
for the good of the habitat and fishermen
who may come after, we let it off the hook.

We've been hearing the same arguments since Appomattox.

Words are only light; what's needed now is fire
to finally end the Civil War and rid ourselves
of anti-federalist, state's rights fundamentalists.

The older generation won't like it
but this older generation is the problem
we will solve by federalizing New York state's tuition-free
college proposal so kids can stay in state
and get a university education or travel
to New York, California, Michigan and get
an out-of-state education for the same cost.

Kids will leave the South and the country will blend,
diversify as kids from Brooklyn, Bloomfield Hills
and Brentwood, happy to get away from home,
will spend four years in South Carolina,
Mississippi or Arkansas before getting the hell out.

And when native southerners graduate from northern schools
they'll never go back to thinking the planet's 10,000 years old,
or that climate change is liberal propaganda,
or that Jesus rode a pterodactyl,
or that corporations are people who deserve voting rights,
or that Deist rhetoric of the Founding Fathers presupposes they intended
        the United States to be a Christian nation in perpetuity,
or that economic segregation is not planned segregation,

or that a free market will regulate itself,

or that there's no need for Black Entertainment Television since there's

> no White Entertainment Television as though ABC, CBS, Fox and NBC
> are not a monopolized White Entertainment Television conglomerate
> where sitcoms set in New York City lack any black actors much less
> characters,

or that one's sexual history dictates one's sexual identity,

or that the NRA isn't a business front for a terrorist organization,

or that feminism is an encroachment on male sovereignty,

or that the confederate flag is suitable to present anywhere

> other than in a rebel museum or a Dixie Land cemetery.

Year of the Chewable Ambien Tab

Luck these days is living longer than the ones you love.
Shulie Firestone died days before her body was discovered
and the killer hiding in the backyard boat is just a kid.
A single pair of running shoes hangs from the stoplight wire.

Shulie Firestone died days before her body was discovered.
She once refused to sweep her father's hall or the offices of NOW.
Another pair of running shoes hangs from the stoplight wire.
It's impossible to decipher their meaning; even footnotes have footnotes.

Refusing to sweep our shared rooms or office now,
my wife sees the Golden Gate Bridge as a high point of modern
     aesthetics.
It's impossible to decipher her reasoning; even her footnotes have
     footnotes.
She's like a bee to a bursting bloom or a WASP to Ralph Lauren.

I consider the Golden Gate Bridge looming in the fog as a monument
     to suicide
while my daughter sings *It's a Beautiful World, a Beautiful World.*
She's a WASP in bloom, bursting with Ralph Lauren.
I planned my burial days after she was born.

My daughter sings *It's a Beautiful World, a Beautiful World.*
The killer hiding in the backyard boat is someone's kid.
I tell my wife to bury me where I was born
since luck these days is living longer than the ones you love.

Mosquito Fleet

Like colored matches swirled in an eddy,
we collect in bunches in Elliott
Bay. A thousand kayak Davids ready
to down Shell's Goliath oil rig, see its
hydraulic pumps ignited by gadfly
harpoons. We're here because the whaling rights
of native Alaskans can't be denied
and polar bears aren't migrating to fight
but our paddles rest on cockpit covers
like candles unlit, like wishes unwished,
when we receive a call from our mother
who asks what we hope to accomplish,
what time she should expect us back
and if we borrowed our father's kayak.

Service Industry Complaints

My daughter drops her bag at the door,
kicks one shoe into the kitchen,
the other into the back door screen and collapses
on the couch as though pushed
and before I can protest Rachel Maddow's face is replaced
by the face of a celebrity I'm too old to recognize.

My daughter complains about the second day
of her new job at the restaurant, how people are disgusting
and leave messes behind them as if the world
is here to pick up after them, as if earning less
than three dollars an hour and whatever tips they leave
means she should thank them for making their table a toilet.

She sounds like Thoreau without the rich friends
as she laments how unjust society is, that some are born
into labor. *If we didn't need money we wouldn't have to work
at all,* she says, as if capitalism is my fault,
the free market my design. *You don't understand,*
she says, *what it's like to stand on your feet all day*
as though I was born into money
and parenting isn't a service industry.

When I tell her she sounds pretentious
she says *that's because I'm better than you.*

World Forgetting by World Forgot

After explaining how Sofia's hair was orange
not red, my three-year-old son begins to lecture
Sofia's mother on the differences between
dragons and dinosaurs while I share a beer
with Syed as he grills onions, vegan burgers
and kosher hotdogs in his backyard.

He tries to explain how the Women's March poster
of the woman wearing the American flag hijab
can be considered both liberal and conservative.
I listen closely because I want it to make sense
but Robbie interrupts with a line from Bob Kaufman.

Syed thinks Robbie's talking about Andy Kaufman
and does a lame Elvis lip and hip impersonation.
I ask if Bob Kaufman's the guy who directed
Eternal Sunshine of the Spotless Mind where
Kirsten Dunst quotes Alexander Pope but calls him
Pope Alexander. Robbie gives us the finger
before leaving to join Jamie and Lucy's discussion
about the new James Baldwin documentary
I Am Not Your Negro. Jamie claims Baldwin's
Sonny Liston article floats like a butterfly
while Norman Mailer's stings like a bee.

Melissa shows my wife a picture of her brother
when he was four years old, insisting,
Tell me that doesn't look exactly like my son,
while my preteen daughter lies on a lounge chair
ignoring us all, her legs extended like the necks
of excavators. She's busy converting the final scene
of *Full Metal Jacket* into a gif on her iPhone,

clipping it where American soldiers march
through burning rubble, their dirty faces lit by the sweat
of fire, singing *The Mickey Mouse Club* theme,
spelling out "Mickey Mouse" letter by single letter.

I hear my son tell Sofia's mother he doesn't have
ten fingers. I watch him lift his palms to her face.
I only have eight, he says. *These two are thumbs.*

Butterfly Wings

My wife's the love child of Pee-wee Herman
and Cindy Crawford, an earnest sensuality
licking the feet of her cackling humor.
She's Allie MacGraw in the motel scene
from *The Getaway* while I'm constantly
auditioning for the role of Steve McQueen.
I've adopted a nut, seed and fruit diet
but still resemble Gene Wilder more.

I shop for sports bras at Old Navy
with our 10-year-old daughter,
blast *Girl, You'll Be a Woman Soon*
driving home with the windows down.
I told my wife I won't fold her laundry
when I can no longer differentiate between
her underpants and those our daughter wears.

When my daughter says she's fat
I tell her she needs to stop paying attention
to media presentations of female beauty.
It's these women's jobs to be cover-ready
two weeks after delivering twins.
I could airbrush myself into a beautiful woman.
If you could afford enough plastic surgery
you can look like the plastic surgery version
of anyone. *Just manage your diet,* I tell her.

When we get home I text my wife she's lucky
our son didn't go swimming at camp today.
When I empty his backpack and unroll
his dry towel one of her thongs falls out.

On Having Two Gynecologists in the Family

It's great to have last-minute prescriptions
filled without appointment, three month's worth
of NuvaRing samples arrive in the mail,
a calm voice at 4 a.m. tells you after
your water breaks to *Relax. Have a glass
of wine. Take a hot bath.* But at one point,
you start receiving angry calls from parents
of your daughter's friends who say
your daughter replied to their daughter's
claim that they came from their mother's
belly with: *I came from my mom's vagina.*
She's four. The phone keeps ringing.
My father says to talk to a pediatrician.
My brother suggests trying private school.

Defending Implants

I try to talk Rebecca out of buying tits,
of allowing men to dictate her value
and identity but, she says, it's hard being a woman
over forty even with an education and sense
of self. Men can only be initially attracted
to what they see; conversation can't grab
a man's attention in crowded bars.
Sometimes you have to blind them
with your headlights and if it's easy
as surgery and stashing stacks of cash
beneath floorboards for months, why not?

Europeans laugh about America's obsession
with breasts, I tell her, and see it as evidence
of juvenile thinking. We're constantly searching
to feed from the comfort of our mother's bosom.
If you purchase boobs, I tell Rebecca,
you'll become a cartoon. What men will want
is something not you. When men compliment
women on their dress, the women often blush
and take it personally as though they sewed
the hem, designed the pattern. If men comment
on your implants they may as well claim
to like your iPhone case or accordion.

It's sort of like a bait and switch, she says.
I can't sell a product if customers never
enter my store. I have to bring them in
with something hanging in the window.
But I own the store. I decide what's for sale.
And I'm just more open, now, as to the currency
I accept. It no longer has to be love.

Acts of Barbery

The lady cutting my hair asks if I watch *Game of Thrones*
so I say the thing that bothers me the most about the show

is not the naked women—though being father to a girl has changed
my views on random nudes—or that the show arranges

to expose at least two sets of nipples every episode. It's the lack
of pubic hair. I accept the show is fantasy with dragons, black

ghosts, red-headed seers marauding through green and grassy plains
but in a time lacking electricity, proper sewage draining

systems or penicillin it's hard to believe so many women
have so little or such sculpted pubic hair. Here is when

the barber next to us interjects that Egyptians
groomed their privates using mixtures of sugar, lemon

and water in a process called sugaring, an early form of Brazilian wax.
Historians cannot agree on eye color, lip symmetry, curve of nose,
      any facts

about the face of Cleopatra yet apparently there's evidence of attendants
shaping the pharaoh's little curlies into a tightly fashioned phalanx.

Is this evidence that history's regressive rather than progressive?
      Were landing
strips present in the Dark Ages? Did Ming Dynasty concubines brand

lovely triangles between their imperial legs? Would Spanish anarchists
or Russian nihilists allow tweezing, accept shaving, endure the twists

and rips of waxing? Are the bushes of 1970s America liberal
protest or conservative reform? Older Jewish cultural

belief states a shaven scalp signals mourning but can today's women
of Zion allow Hitler's mustache to camp above the fountain

from which the messiah may spring? Named Sexiest Woman of 2013
Gwyneth Paltrow confessed on *Ellen* she shaved herself clean

down there and looks like a girl of eight. Delilah waits
as Samson slumbers, gripping her scissors, drawing the shades.

Bathroom Bill

I'm the straight, white guy who's seen *Pink Flamingos*
in its entirety and attended multiple Halloween showings

of *The Rocky Horror Picture Show* so when I walked by
the line the length of a dragon's tail extending out the ladies' room

at the Convention Center in Washington DC and noticed
the hand-drawn unisex sign taped over the plastic silhouette

of the ghost-like version of the human male, I strode right in
excited to participate in the progressive social act of defying

gender assignments but no one in the bathroom would make eye
     contact
with me. The women walked straight to the stalls and locked

the door, making me feel like a predator, like I misinterpreted
the unisex sign and it meant only women. But there were urinals.

And I've been to stadium bathrooms where there's standing water
on the floor, sink taps running until they overflow and urinal lines

ten deep. There's singing and beer drinking and "if you shake it
more than twice you're just playing with it" and laughter and fights

and dudes who stand right next to you even if there's a whole row
not being used. I've writ my name in snow, on library walls,

on police cruiser tires. Once I put out a camp fire and engaged
in full conversations about Ezra Pound's WWII radio speeches,

the one-eyed pyramid on the dollar bill literally representing the pyramid scheme at the root economic value of our currency

and whether the quarterback should retire from the game completely
after that third quarter sack. I've stood there so long I've actually
    thought

about how long I was standing there planning and reciting
exactly what to say when I return to the table if the conversation

hasn't changed since I left it. But maybe I got the whole thing wrong.
Maybe unisex restrooms are designed for us to be comfortable

with the space designated for sharing, not with whom we share it.

43

Galileo Looking Up

> Galileo was trying to build a scientific method in a world
> based more on books than on nature . . . more on closing
> one's eyes than on observing through the telescope.
>
> —Rossella Gigli

When confronted with the discovery
of water on Mars and the possibility
of extraterrestrial life, rather than shrinking
away like Galileo before the Roman Inquisition,
Pope John Paul suggested that if Martians exist,
we must introduce them to Jesus.

Galileo proved man's the center
of the universe by retreating
from his own evidence of heliocentrism
when confronted with excommunication.

It's impossible not to consider Galileo's
choice of life over truth while walking
in Florence beneath a moon still called
the moon as if it were the only one—
as if Saturn doesn't claim more than sixty,
most of them named from classical myth.

The highest points of the Arno flood remain
stained on the bricks of the Duomo walls.

Inside the Museum of the History of Science,
Galileo's middle finger, encased in glass,
forever extends towards heaven.

Jesus Isn't Licensed; He Can't Take the Wheel

Atheists deserve a lane reserved for them on state highways.
Remove the signage signifying "High Occupancy Vehicle" and replace

with signs reading "Atheists Only." State troopers could verify
atheist drivers by permit stickers shaped like Nietzsche's silhouette

or by "There Is No God" specialty license plates issued
by the state. If my Jewish daughter's public school requires

she attend on Passover and fasting Muslim students must sit
dry-mouthed in my classes during Ramadan, the least

Christians can do is wait. They have all the time in this world
and the next. I live across the street from Our Mother of Perpetual Traffic

and every Sunday I make illegal left turns, intentionally cutting
off the line of cars queuing into the church's parking lot.

Sometimes they honk. But I'm the one who's impatient.
Eternity closes early and, on Sunday, so does the grocery store.

Easter, 2012

My daughter picks the painted eggs
from under the juniper bushes that line
the path as maples weep last night's rain
and the sun apologizes for being absent.
My daughter's dress looks like the flag
of Finland. Her favorites eggs are the ones
farthest under the wet whorls of needles.
She never looks where she reaches but turns
her head as though her sight's a handicap
and only touch can be trusted when elbow
deep. My wife and I sit on the wood-warped
bench, holding hands for the first time in months
and protecting the jellybean nest from other
girls and boys who run through the park
tripping over stuffed baskets, foil-wrapped
chocolate kisses erupting everywhere
like parents' laughter. Behind our bench,
the river hungers, cracking ice along
the shore like formerly broken, finally
healed fingers breaking through a plaster cast.

Kris Kringle's Picture on a Coca-Cola Can

After hanging plastic candy canes,
shatterproof Santas and half a dozen
pine-scented sticks from our artificial
Douglas fir; my Jewish daughter turns
the seventh bulb on the electric menorah
in her bedroom window while across
the hall my infant son sleeps beneath
a ceiling of golden stars projected
by his penguin-shaped Dream Lite,
the sound machine filling his room
with ocean waves and their crashing.

Faithless and Virtue-less Night

I tell my students about the movie *Her* where Joaquin Phoenix plays
a denizen of sometime-in-the-future Los Angeles who grows
to love his new operating system voiced by Scarlett Johansson.
They fall in love and fall apart like any relationship.
I use this film to illustrate irony, describing how the human lacks
emotional connections with other humans, how Johansson's voice cracks
as her technology breaks under the weight of this new emotional life
like a roof collapsing beneath an unexpected April snow.

Despite Best Picture and Best Screenplay nominations,
despite Joaquin Phoenix having been nominated for five Academy Awards,
despite Scarlett Johansson's face covering magazines
even when she's not promoting anything; my students never heard
of this film. So I list a number of the director's previous titles.

I summarize *Being John Malkovich,* saying it's about a couple working
on the eleventh-and-a-half floor in a Manhattan office building
where they hunch down the hallways and discover a portal
behind a filing cabinet that delivers them into the head of John Malkovich
where they inhabit Malkovich's body until they're spit out
on the shoulder of the New Jersey Turnpike. I admit it's totally weird
but my students look at me like I directed this film instead of Spike Jonze;
like I wrote it, not Charlie Kaufman; as if being in the audience consuming
art makes you part of it, makes you guilty in the conspiracy of its making.

I've started lining my office wall with rejection letters, taped
my favorites like crowns behind my computer screen, so when I work
the handwritten addendums scribbled on the bottoms
of the standard forms remind me that I'm *not writing poetry,*
that I should *try prose,* that *there's not enough poetic moments* in my work
as though it's me and not the world lacking *poetic moments.* I wish
my world did not contain Netflix, TruckNutz, or Tom Brokaw

on the radio complaining how every new iPhone demands the purchase
of new cords and chargers to fit the adjusted plug. He warns
that whatever society follows ours will condemn us for our useless
and outdated cords stuffed like old shoestrings in kitchen drawers.

If I wasn't busy debating my school's tech specialist
over how Smart TVs can't be that intelligent if they still require
human fingers to command them via remote control buttons;
I could practice reading my poems in a British accent, raising
my inflection at the end of every line as if it was a question, dropping
adjectives across my pages like little seeds of obfuscation blooming
into some fruit that's vaguely delicious but devoid of any food value.
These are the empty calories in the corn chips, the chemical flavor tricking
your tongue to tell your brain it tastes cheese when it's only the imitation
of cheese constructed to last on the shelf and not even expire
in your stomach. I refuse to write *Faithful and Virtuous Night.*
Why insult the sunset by calling it merely *beautiful?* It's like making
a comic book movie and hiring Jessica Alba to play
the Invisible Girl or casting Scarlett Johansson in a science fiction picture
at the height of her beauty and only using her voice.

A Matter of Tides

I've been writing poems for close to twenty
years and even those that bought my book
admit to never reading it when I
ask. I don't give my older work a look
either. My cousin spends hours mixing crème
fraîche in his kitchen to serve with stuffed quail
which his family devours like they're condemned.
All his work gone like the western gray whale.
It's hard to look at Thimble Island homes,
their stilts perching them upon the rocks, and
not see how the tide left the line of foam
behind. And tides return. On Kelsey Beach,
my daughter says, of some granite I found,
it's beautiful and flings it in the Sound.

Afternoon with a Plutocrat

After spending the day trolling Long Island Sound
on my wife's cousin's forty-foot boat, *Liquid Assets,*
my daughter asks about his job, how he got the boat
and I listen to his attempt to articulate
to a seven-year-old how American investment strategies
can manipulate international economies.

When he mentions markets she lifts her sunglasses
and wants to know if the market he works
in is like the one in Disney's *Aladdin,* loud with vendors
and farm animals and monkeys wearing fezzes.

This is where I chirp in and mention the difference
between the market where Princess Jasmine's caught
stealing and where he works is no one loses a hand
for lifting apples in his market. My wife's cousin smiles,
reminds us that Jasmine was going to be punished
until she revealed her face before the palace guards
who dropped to their knees like fallen swords.

My daughter's bored. It's obvious she stopped
listening. She presses her fingers into the burnt skin
of her left arm and watches, when she lifts
her hand, the white ovals of her fingerprints retreat
into redness like conscripted soldiers paid
to fight but not committed to shedding blood.

Everything Must Go

I thought my job as father was to protect
my kids from pain so when my grandmother died
we didn't bring my daughter to the funeral.
We didn't tell her about my uncles dying until she asked
almost two years later when she was on the raft
with my cousins in the middle of an Ohio pond.

So I blame myself for her expression now: caught
in that shocked pause before hysteria
in the parking lot of Sports Authority three days
before it closes for good. She's almost nine and this is
only the second time we've shopped here.
Last month, everything was half off. We bought
a Rawlings catcher's mitt for $30 to give her brother
and a pair Under Armour soccer cleats for 25.

Now, three days before the liquidation ends
everything's slashed. Socks for a quarter.
Titanium lacrosse poles and Louisville bats, light
as tooth picks, cut to ten and forty bucks respectively.
Elbow pads for four bucks. The racks themselves
for sale. The shelving. Mirrors stripped off dressing room walls.

But I wonder if I've done more harm than good
by shielding my daughter from loss as we watch
other scavengers picking at this free-market carcass, skinning
it clean like starved cannibals as the store's automatic doors chomp
open and closed and a couple loads their flatbed truck
with mannequin parts: arms, legs and headless torsos.

My Daughter's Teeth, My Father's Beard

My daughter wants to lose her teeth.
All her friends have: Gavin, Gabi,
Brooke and Morgan, Samantha, Matt,
Rebecca and Riley. She's started
banging into doorjambs mouth first.
I tell her to wait. Her new teeth
will grow in when they're ready.

I began to shave when I turned
twelve. I had no hair but lathered
with my father's cream. The razor
slid across my face as smoothly
as a skater at Olympic trials.

My father shaved like a plowman:
digging trenches; dragging blades;
pulling unwanted, stubborn weeds;
annoyed by all he had to do
again, again, by another
season gone, another on its way.

Career Girl

My sister warns me to watch the Barbie
influence on my daughter. Body image
develops early. She doesn't like see-
ing girls imitate the plastic visage
of beauty, that breasts should swell like balloons,
that legs should extend into the throat, that
hair must be blond and yet this afternoon
my daughter paced the toy store aisle cat-
like, deciding between surfer Barbie
and president Barbie, race car Barbie
and astronaut Barbie, pilot Barbie,
doctor Barbie and scientist Barbie.
And though I agree with my sister's fears,
my daughter picks Barbies based on career.

The Tail

My daughter's favorite film is Disney's *Little Mermaid,*
which I'm afraid instructs her the point of her existence
is to marry and to accomplish this she must sacrifice
her identity, give up her fin, erase her voice from the equation.

After years of listening to her beg for a mermaid tail,
after swimming lessons and proving she can tread
in the deep on her own for minutes at a time, my wife
and I concede, surprise her with one for her seventh birthday.
She immediately pulls it on and hops to the car
like a real mermaid up the beach after a scrambling crab.

The older girls at our local pool swarm my daughter
on the steps, adoring her as if she arrived on half shell.
Every compliment they pay her: *It's awesome; so cool;*
I'll trade you for my little brother she accepts personally.
She describes the process of selecting the blue and green scale
pattern, demonstrates how the triangle of industrial plastic fits
in the fabric below her feet to power her butterfly kick.

On the other side of the pool, two girls lean against the wall.
The girl with pigtails mumbles how my daughter should
be embarrassed of all this attention as the other girl swims
away to join the others at the altar of my mermaid daughter,
leaving the pigtail girl to pout like a celebrity abandoned
by fame. The pigtail girl paddles to the deep end and climbs
the ladder slowly like some new weight's been added
to her suit. She tells her parents she wants to go home
before lifting a towel to dry off, starting with her legs.

Another Wild Animal

No one wants to read a straight
man's writing on women my second
wave feminist mother tells me.
No matter the intent she says *it all*
reads like misogyny yet what can
one do but question the significance
of the vagina when living with wife
and daughter, when both father
and brother are practicing OBGYNs?

The mohel held my hand that held
the blade that circumcised my son
and now I'm learning things I didn't
know about the penis: foreskin
treatment, scrotum care, the need
to cover when changing diapers
to prevent urine spraying everywhere.

In the backyard my daughter waters
her strawberries with my mother
but when she drops the garden hose
it kicks in squirts across the grass,
ducking from their grabbing hands
like some wild animal showing
its teeth, refusing domestication.

Rubber Rain Boots

My daughter, like a specter of death, climbs
onto my bed to wish me a happy birthday.
Her face is like her mother's. She's lucky.
She's also magic. She mutes alarm clocks
just by pointing at them. When she points
I hit the sleep button, not ready to commit
to the day. My daughter says when I was younger
she was my mother and my mother's mother
when she was younger. She says her brother
was my father but she doesn't have a brother.
I ask about her grandfather, who, she says,
is also her brother's son. So I am fatherless
like my father on my birthday and each woman
in my life is my mother. Then my daughter
claims she's like a snake: she's changed
from her pajamas, like a snake that's shed
its skin and sits between the pillows, thumb
in mouth, like Buddha in pink tutu and rubber rain boots.

In the backyard, the neighbor kids kill
each other with their plastic guns.

Summer's Thousand Appetites

My grandma died an hour after power
went out along the Delmarva Peninsula.
She told my sister life was like a single
deep breath. Should we wash her lipstick off
her coffee cup? Erase her voice from
our answering machine? Who's in charge
of her trust now? It wasn't until selecting
flowers for the funeral I actually cried,
the idea of roses or lilies drying in July
with summer's thousand appetites licking
away their fragrance, tossing crisp petals
across the headstones. The last I saw
my grandma she was in bed, blowing
me kisses with both hands as if she stood
on the deck of a Mediterranean-bound
cruise ship, leaving me alone on the dock,
which rocked and heaved in the ship's wake
long after it pulled out of the harbor
and was swallowed by the horizon.

Waking

In the parking lot, a wake of turkey vultures picks
at the raccoon carcass's skin with pointed beaks.

The brightest section of sidewalk is the square
beside the stairwell where the suicide landed, where

the school hired a power washing crew to clean
the stain instead of funding a memorial. Rain

falls. A single engine plane takes off behind the fence.

The Whistle and the Scream

I understand you think everything
changes, that evolution is positively
tuned, that even parking lot pavements
contain aspects of aesthetic beauty
in their cracks and I'm not claiming
you should care about a family
of polar bears stuck on a single
shard of ice in the arctic but you never
sat on the beach at Walden Pond
in August as the lifeguard slept
on her stand behind sunglasses
while three able swimmers slipped
under the buoyed safety rope
and raced out to the center
as their younger brother kicked
behind them but couldn't keep up.

I can't recall which was louder:
the whistle or the screams.

Suicide at Seven

I asked for her bike after she declared
she'd kill herself for what her parents did.
Then she lay in the middle of the spoon-end
of our newly blacktopped cul-de-sac,
her arms outstretched, legs apart, head
uplifted in the Mississippi sun. I observed
from the curb as a single neighborhood car
slowed to swing wide around her, the driver
stretching over the passenger side to warn
out his half-opened window to play
in our yards, not in the street. I watched
her like Saturday morning cartoons until
dinner lights from kitchen windows framed
still lifes in painted shadows across the dry
Biloxi lawns; until my butt hurt from sitting
on the sidewalk cement which was cracked
and lifted like some municipal hangnail
by roots of the giant oak tree which was split,
sometime last summer, by a lightning strike.

Daughter Taking Selfie

Whenever I believe in individuality
I'm confronted by my grandfather's captain photo
from the '46 Michigan football team hanging
in my office. His face is my face: extended
forehead, lips swollen as if stung, the nose appearing
broken but, despite playing in leather helmets
lacking facemasks, never was.

Whenever I consider any iconoclasm
unique, I recall my ancestor expelled
from Oxford for presenting anti-Catholic
dissertations or the one who abandoned
his Royal Navy post, turned pirate
and died of syphilis in the Caribbean.

When I collect my daughter from school
she asks to see my phone so she can take
another selfie wearing her mother's necklace
which all her fellow classmates loved.

When I ask about her day she says they watched
a jungle video and her teacher asked
Wouldn't it be fun to be a monkey?
which caused her arm to rise almost, she claims,
by instinct and submit to her kindergarten class:
We were all monkeys before.

And we live in the South, only miles away
from the Creation Museum where a girl farms
beside a velociraptor in one of the exhibits
as if history's a thing happening all at once.

Closing Time

We've been together nearly twenty years
and you've become a European tourist
destination. Galleria Nazionale d'Arte Antica
is closed Tuesdays. Bang all you want
on the bolted door but *Judith Beheading
Holofernes* won't be revealed. Shake
the Parisian gates of Luxembourg Gardens
during lunch; you won't get in. Caretakers
siesta from noon to some-vague-time
until they finally bore of themselves and return
to work, enjoying every grunt from each
American whose knees have gone stiff
from waiting, back numb after curb-squatting
for the last hour, tearing through what was left
of their breakfast baguette and souvenir
chocolates they planned on taking home as gifts.

My arrival was once anticipated
like a holiday: trees trimmed with lights
along the boulevard, fresh flowers cut
to carpet floors, every opening
a celebration of music and dance.

I always left donations in the bowl,
was kind to girls behind the ticket counters,
smiled at guards who instructed me to remove
my hat and keep my shoulders covered.

Now the only lights I see are above
the exit, writ in foreign letters I can't
understand. But I accept the blame.
I never took time to learn the language.

Delayed Gratification

My friend who recently divorced
his wife of fifteen years tells me
about the woman he's dating now
who's teaching him Tantric meditation.
He claims to be having the best sex
of his life yet he's not experienced
orgasm in close to seven months.

I tell him when my wife and I share
a day off during the week we drive
to the outlets and shop for sales.
She tries on dresses for which she lacks
occasions to wear. I slide my feet
in hundred dollar loafers and glide
around the store like I'm the boss
of something. We never buy anything.

Sometimes even, after midnight,
my wife will catch me in my office
hypnotized by the glow of the Apple's
glare, my Amazon shopping cart
full to the point of free shipping
but I follow her to bed without hitting
Pay Now before the screen shuts off
and the computer puts itself to sleep.

Straight Shooting

After an avocado and banana breakfast
on Oligarch Avenue we cross the street
to Proletariat Place for Bloody Marys
and mimosas where Brian says the best
two days of a boater's life are the day
they buy the boat and the day they sell it.
It's kind of like marriage, he says. He worries
about identifying as a bisexual at this stage
of his life though. He doesn't want to be
married anymore, at least not to his wife,
but what if this is just a phase? What if
what he enjoys now isn't what he'll enjoy
in ten years and he blew up his life chasing
pleasure as 40 holds the door for 50 before
60 slams it on this sad sack with a Cialis prescription?
How can he know if this is who he really is?
Daphne asks if prostate-induced orgasms
are really better like Boy George claimed
in an interview. Brian says there's little difference
except you feel it in the very marrow
of your bones. Daphne tells the story of trying
to stick her finger up an old boyfriend
who gripped her wrist with such violence
it shocked her out of her sexual state.
Even while in bed with a woman he believed
the prostate was some gay light switch that can't be
unflipped. Gal wonders if we and our wives
were kidnapped by a man who threatens
to kill us if we refuse to fellate him, would we,
in order to save our wife's life and our own?
Christian says he couldn't. He'd fear
the metaphysical implications. Guy says

it's disgusting. His wife, sitting next to him,
says *it's a penis not broccoli but I'm glad to hear
you find it gross. I'll never do it to you again.*
As Christian unpacks his mistake, Gal looks
at me, says *forget saving lives, how much
would it take for you to give a man head?
Would a million dollars be enough? A billion?*
What else can I do but shrug, admit *I'd have to ask
my wife.* She handles all negotiations on our behalf.

Streaking through the Fire

When they raid the house we're doing nothing.
Michelle makes sure I'm quiet, leads me
through the kitchen crowd, out the back door,
across the porch and through the side gate
until we're on the sidewalk like lovers strolling
through innocent night; too old to be guilty
of anything; pretending to debate whether copper
should be considered brown or that sea-foam shade
of statues crowning fountains in Italian piazzas.
She questions why we're running from the air-quote
scene of the crime since those cops could be cops
or just regular dudes dressed as police for Halloween
and I wonder if police aren't always only people
pretending to be cops; the colors of their uniforms bleeding
into their skin, transforming their identities
on the cellular level down to their very DNA.
When she insists I'm *preaching to the choir*
I think she says I'm *streaking through the fire*
which makes me want to hold her hand but I've learned
nothing ruins the beauty of flame like touching.

Something Sinister

You believe an elegant God punishes
our truancy by slipping the only stoplight
in a six-mile radius into something more
comfortable, something sinister and red.

Before calling you selfish, narcissistic,
solipsistic and reminding you the world
is full of life and dying and every second
packed with death, you detail how Philip's
father's second wife died last week during
voluntary cosmetic surgery and some girl
you know at work, her brother was killed
by an oncoming truck heading the wrong
way on an early morning highway and since
things come in threes there must be another
death waiting out there like some bored sniper
scouring Mardi Gras' crowd through his scope.

Stalks of corn along the road stretch
long shadows toward us, as though night
itself attempts to grab our bumper, drag us in.

When Robert Johnson comes on the radio,
I swear only Vishnu has more hands.

City Sleeping Late

The geometry of guilt is impossible to establish
and each New Year's Eve, people are killed, struck
down by handgun fire, ammunition shot into the air
in celebration of another year gone, another year
beginning. These shots are more than just bangs.
The bullets eventually arch through the atmosphere
and return to earth, gain momentum and travel
through windshields, billboards, balcony gardens,
skulls. Those struck drop, deflating like inflatable dolls dancing
outside car dealerships until they're unplugged and empty
with a shrug. Death can be delivered from outside
the city limits, from the apartment building across the street
or from three counties over. On New Year's it's hard to tell
who passed out in the hallway, who fell over the loveseat,
who suffered cardiac arrest before the ball dropped
and who was touched by God or the Fates or the Furies
until morning. Even then, no one wakes to watch
the sun's early shapes constructed upon the walls or read
yesterday's obituaries in today's paper or consider
how unlikely we are to be born at all, much less in a society that uses
forks, laces shoes, showers daily, computerizes dating,
freezes sperm. It's statistically improbable that we'll live
to next year. Just as improbable is the likelihood of us touching
as the stars wink themselves to death; of your sleeping breath washing
over my chin as the moon, curved like a clipped nail, fades
into the sky's whitening carpet; of us waking together
to weigh breakfast options in a city sleeping late.

Urban Pejorative

My friend condemns suburban life, insists
each activity centers around a purchase.
He accuses my entire area code and those like it
of being one extended drive-thru mall sustaining
the occasional soccer field, bike lane, dog park.
How can any culture subsist among planned
communities and droplets of houses sharing
identical floor plans? According to my friend,
I've voluntarily doomed myself to spending
a lifetime trapped in a department store elevator.

I admit there are minivan lovers here.
They'll sell you on it if you tease them.
It's all about the space, they'll tell you,
the luxury of having that extra room.

My friend talks about New York as if he spends
every autumn weekend attending lectures
at the 92nd Street Y; as if his own apartment building
doesn't sprout from the head of a Duane Reade;
as if Manhattan Island isn't a 13-mile-long bodega
sinking beneath the weight of its dry cleaners,
pizza stands and Times Square; as if because he lives
seven subway stops from the Met that he's won
some Coolness War he's waged against me for years.

Now I'll admit you can find anything in the city
(a row of Shea Stadium upper deck seats,
a first edition *On the Road,* a Birkin bag
from '84 autographed by Serge Gainsbourg)
but other than that New York City street-grit
that sticks like dried sweat to exposed skin

you can't carry any of it home. Your apartment's
too small. The bathroom door opens into the toilet.
The kitchen sink's in the hall. Your bed doubles
as your couch. Your closet's already overfull
and you only own two pairs of running shoes.
Plus, as my friend's landlord just reminded him,
the freight elevator's only available Sunday
and the next available reservation isn't until spring.

Late Night Not Early Morning

I can't recall if it really happened, if what I see
is memory or imagery seeded by his retelling
but life, then, was a blinking yellow light
we accelerated though. Where were the parents
that owned the homes we'd trash? John Gallagher knew
my penchant for jumping out of windows, lifting
handles of cars parked along York Road, flicking
cigarette butts at police officers, so he saw
the mistake Luther made by bragging his father kept
a gun upstairs. After a race halfway up
the staircase, John caught me by my flannel shirt,
dragged me over the banister and cracked me
across the jaw. Which stopped me dead.
He claims I thanked him as I followed him

back to the porch to bum a couple cigarettes
off his girlfriend and question why *after midnight*
is called *early morning* considering it's still
dark and so much can happen before first light.

AUTHOR ACKNOWLEDGMENTS

The author is grateful to the editors of the publications where poems first appeared or are set to appear: *The American Journal of Poetry, The Antioch Review, Atlanta Review, Big Muddy, Blast Furnace, Blue Mesa Review, Blue River Review, Breakwater Review, Columbia Poetry Review, Exposition Review, Fugue, Gargoyle, Gravel, Gulf Stream, Harpur Palate, Hayden's Ferry Review, Into the Void, Iodine, Iron Horse Literary Review, J Journal, Lunch Ticket, Natural Bridge, New Delta Review, New Madrid, Owen Wister Review, OxMag, PANK, Pembroke Magazine, Peregrine, Permafrost, Poet Lore, Portland Review, Salamander, Rattle, The RavensPerch, Saw Palm, Steam Ticket, Switchback, Tampa Review, Tar River Poetry, Toad Suck Review, Willow Springs,* and *Yemassee.*

SERIES ACKNOWLEDGMENTS

We at Wheelbarrow Books have many people to thank without whom *Smuggling Elephants through Airport Security* would never be in your hands. We begin by thanking all those writers who submitted manuscripts to the fifth Wheelbarrow Books Prize for Poetry. We want to single out the finalists, Jeanine Hathaway, Erin Murphy, Derek Sheffield, and Arne Weingart, whose manuscripts moved and delighted us and which we passed on to the judge, along with Brad Johnson's, for her final selection. That judge, Carolyn Forché, we thank for her thoughtful selection of the winner and her critical comments offered earlier in this book.

Our thanks to Lydia Barron, Grace Carras, Allison Costello, Cindy Hunter Morgan, Amy Potchen, Estee Schlenner, Elizabeth Sauter, Alexis Stark, and Arzelia Williams for their careful reading of manuscripts and insightful commentary on their selections, and especially to Laurie Hollinger, assistant director at the RCAH Center for Poetry, who also read the manuscripts and provided the logistical aid and financial wizardry for this project. Sarah Teppen, a previous RCAH Center for Poetry intern, designed our Wheelbarrow Books logo which makes us smile every time we see it.

We go on to thank Stephen Esquith, dean of the Residential College in the Arts and Humanities, who has given his continued support to the RCAH Center for Poetry and Wheelbarrow Books since their inception. As we began thinking seriously about Wheelbarrow Books, conversation with June Youatt, provost at Michigan State University, was encouraging and MSU Press director Gabriel Dotto and assistant director/editor-in-chief Julie Loehr were eager to support the efforts of poets to reach an eager audience. We cannot thank them enough for having faith in us, and a love of literature, to collaborate on this project.

Thanks to our current editorial board, Sarah Bagby, Mark Doty, George Ellenbogen, Carolyn Forché, Thomas Lynch, George Ella Lyon and Naomi Shihab Nye for believing Wheelbarrow Books a worthy undertaking and lending their support and their time to our success.

Finally, to our patrons: without your belief in the Wheelbarrow Books Poetry Series and your generous financial backing we would still be sitting around the conference table adding up our loose change. You are making it possible for poets who have never had a book of poetry published, something that's becoming harder and harder these days with so many presses discontinuing their publishing of poetry, to find an outlet for their work. You are also supporting the efforts of established poets to continue to reach a large and grateful audience. We name you here with great admiration and appreciation:

Beth Alexander	Jean Kruger	Patricia and Robert Miller
Mary Hayden		Brian Teppen

WHEELBARROW BOOKS

Anita Skeen, *Series Editor*

Sarah Bagby	George Ellenbogen	Thomas Lynch
Mark Doty	Carolyn Forché	Naomi Shihab Nye

Wheelbarrow Books, established in 2016, is an imprint of the RCAH Center for Poetry at Michigan State University, published and distributed by MSU Press. The biannual Wheelbarrow Books Poetry Prize is awarded every year to one emerging poet who has not yet published a first book and to one established poet.

SERIES EDITOR: Anita Skeen, professor in the Residential College in the Arts and Humanities (RCAH) at Michigan State University, founder and past director of the RCAH Center for Poetry, director of the Creative Arts Festival at Ghost Ranch, and director of the Fall Writing Festival

The RCAH Center for Poetry opened in the fall of 2007 to encourage the reading, writing, and discussion of poetry and to create an awareness of the place and power of poetry in our everyday lives. We think about this in a number of ways, including through readings, performances, community outreach, and workshops. We believe that poetry is and should be fun, accessible, and meaningful. We are building a poetry community in the Greater Lansing area and beyond. Our undertaking of the Wheelbarrow Books Poetry Series is one of the gestures we make to aid in connecting good writers and eager readers beyond our regional boundaries. Information about the RCAH Center for Poetry at MSU can be found at http://poetry.rcah.msu.edu and also at https://centerforpoetry.wordpress.com and on Facebook and Twitter (@CenterForPoetry).

The mission of the Residential College in the Arts and Humanities at Michigan State University is to weave together the passion, imagination, humor, and candor of the arts and humanities to promote individual well-being and the common good. Students, faculty, and community partners in the arts and humanities have the power to focus critical attention on the public issues we face and the opportunities we have to resolve them. The arts and humanities not only give us the pleasure of living in the moment but also the wisdom to make sound judgments and good choices.

The mission, then, is to see things as they are, to hear things as others may, to tell these stories as they should be told, and to contribute to the making of a better world. The Residential College in the Arts and Humanities is built on four cornerstones: world history, art and culture, ethics, and engaged learning. Together they define an open-minded public space within which students, faculty, staff, and community partners can explore today's common problems and create shared moral visions of the future. Discover more about the Residential College in the Arts and Humanities at Michigan State at http://rcah.msu.edu.